Inside Ga...

Galaxies consist of stars and t... ...d to make stars.

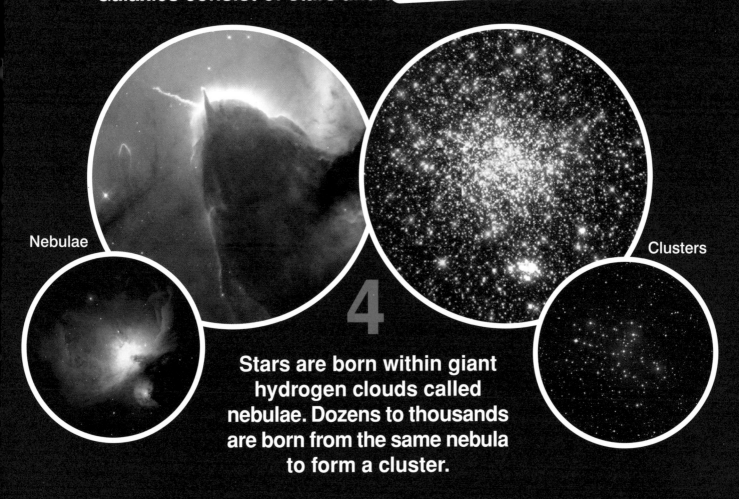

Nebulae

Clusters

4

Stars are born within giant hydrogen clouds called nebulae. Dozens to thousands are born from the same nebula to form a cluster.

Stars eventually die. Some shed their outer atmosphere. Others explode.

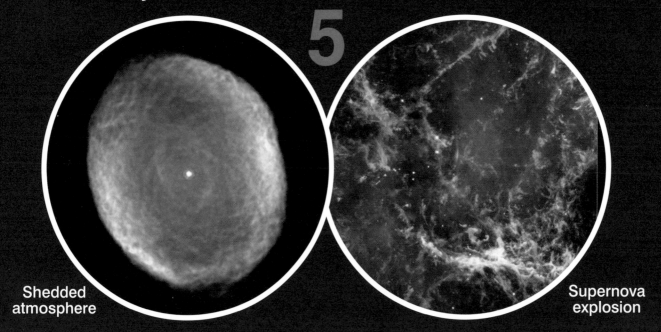

5

Shedded atmosphere

Supernova explosion

Our Galaxy
and the
Universe

Ken Graun

Suzanne Maly

Ken Press

Look up and enjoy the beauty of the heavens.
K. G.

I am deeply grateful to Ken for his dedication and talents,
to my children who have made my life a joy,
and to the many scientists who have shared their knowledge with educators.
S. M. M.

Publisher's Cataloging-in-Publication

Graun, Ken.
  Our galaxy and the universe / Ken Graun, Suzanne
Maly. — 1st ed.
  p. cm. — (21st century astronomy series)

  Includes index.
  LCCN: 2002091126
  ISBN: 1-928771-08-4
  SUMMARY: General overview of the universe including galaxies, the Milky Way,
stars, star clusters, nebulae, black holes, supernovae and more for young readers.

  1. Astronomy — Juvenile literature. 2. Cosmology — Juvenile literature.
3. Astronomy. 4. Cosmology.   I. Maly, Suzanne.   II. Title

QB46.G73 2002   520
                        QBI02-701230

Published by Ken Press, Tucson, Arizona, United States of America ★ www.kenpress.com
Printed in Hong Kong by South Sea International Press Ltd.

1 3 5 7 9 10 8 6 4 2

Introduction & Table of Contents

The authors, surrounded by Ms. Maly's students.

Standing, from left:
Taniya Qureshi,
Ken Graun,
Chris Sinkinson,
Ramesh Smith,
Michel Schwemmer
and Suzanne Maly.

Sitting, from left:
Isobela Georgiades,
Azur Thompson,
and
Vanessa M. Padilla.

The first book in this series explored our solar system and the planets. This book reaches beyond by taking you through our galaxy to the end of the Universe.

The Universe and all its galaxies are larger and more mysterious than anyone ever imagined. It has taken astronomers hundreds of years to piece together a basic understanding of the Universe and it will take many more to fully comprehend it.

The goal of astronomy and all the sciences is to understand the workings of nature. We do this out of curiosity and we do it to help and better ourselves. Our scientific endeavors in the last century have led to incredible insights that have provided us with modern medicines, computers, higher standards of living and a good sense of who we are in this Universe. However, we are still only at the beginning of a long scientific journey. May you join in and take us farther along the path.

The Universe 4
Galaxies 6
Our Milky Way Galaxy 10
The Milky Way Band 12
The Birth of Stars 14
Nebulae & Star Clusters . . . 16
Stars 18
Dying Stars 20
Supernova Deaths 22
Black Holes 24
Electromagnetic Spectrum . 26
Seeing the Universe 29
A Great Mystery 30
Various Ends 31
Glossary 32
Measurements & Index 34

When astronomers peer
deep into the Universe,
beyond the stars of our
Milky Way Galaxy, all they
see are galaxies. This
picture was taken by the orbiting
Hubble Space Telescope. Most of
the specks and blobs in this picture are
galaxies billions of light years from our
Milky Way Galaxy. This picture represents
an area in the sky about the size of this
period (.) held at arm's length.

Location near the
"Big Dipper" where
this picture was taken.

Can You Find...

A few specks in this pic-
ture are stars that can be
identified by their spikes.
How many can you count?
Remember, these stars are
in our Milky Way Galaxy.
They just happen to be in
the direction that this
picture was taken in.

The Universe

The Universe is everything that there is. Astronomers define it as all of space and everything in it. It is very hard to imagine that the Universe came into being at the one instant of the "Big Bang" more than 12 billion years ago. Everything, that is, all matter and energy, came into existence at that moment. And, since matter and energy can neither be created nor destroyed, it is all with us today.

What's in it?

If you held the Universe in your hands and looked at it closely, you would see billions of fuzzy specks. Each of these specks would be a galaxy. A galaxy is a collection of billions of stars. Stars are only formed in galaxies and galaxies have various shapes and sizes. Astronomers estimate that there are about 125 billion of them in our Universe.

How big is it?

Adults have trouble understanding the size of the Universe, so don't be surprised if you can't picture just how big it is!

Before we talk about its size, we need to start with a measurement "stick." Instead of using miles or kilometers, we are going to use light years. A light year is the distance that light travels in one year. In space, light moves at the rate of 186,282 miles per second. How fast is this? Snap your fingers and light has just circled the world more than 7 times. In one year, light travels nearly six trillion miles (6,000,000,000,000). It would take you nearly 9 million years to cover this same distance in a car going 75 miles per hour.

The nearest star to our Sun, Proxima Centauri, is 4.3 light years away. Our galaxy is 100,000 light years in diameter. The Andromeda Galaxy, which is one of our nearest galactic neighbors, is 2.3 million light years away. The Universe stretches for over 12 billion light years in every direction.

Do you know how a million compares to a billion and trillion?

Get this. If you started counting right now to a million, at the rate of one number per second, day and night, it would take you 11.5 days to complete the task. But if you wanted to count to 1 billion, it would take you about 31.7 years. A trillion would take 31,700 years. You better start right now. Wow!

1 million = 1,000,000
1 billion = 1,000,000,000
1 trillion = 1,000,000,000,000

The most distant galaxies that astronomers can see are about 10 billion light years away. The starlight from these galaxies had to travel for 10 billion years before finally reaching Earth.

One-inch scale

How big would the Universe be if the Earth were one inch across? In this case, the Sun would be 978 feet away, the nearest star over 50,000 miles away and the diameter of our galaxy would be one billion miles. The Andromeda Galaxy would be 27 billion miles away, while the Universe would stretch for 73 trillion miles in every direction.

Even this is too much for most of us to imagine, so let's really bring it down to size. If our Milky Way Galaxy were just one inch across, which is the size of a quarter, the Andromeda Galaxy would be a mere 23 inches away, and the Universe would stretch for 2 miles in every direction.

Universe Facts

Age: Between 12 & 16 billion years old.

Beginning: The Universe began from an "explosion" called the *Big Bang*.

Type: Expanding Universe? At this time, astronomers' best guess is that the Universe may exist and expand forever.

Chemical elements in the Universe: 75% hydrogen, 25% helium and traces of all other elements.

Number of galaxies in the Universe: Around 125 billion (125,000,000,000).

SEE INSIDE BACK COVER

The Andromeda Galaxy, which is visible to the naked eye, is one of the closest spiral galaxies. It is located in the direction of the constellation Andromeda, which is visible from September through February. This galaxy is 120,000 light years in diameter and just over 2,300,000 light years away.

A small elliptical galaxy that is gravitationally bound to the Andromeda Galaxy.

Another small elliptical galaxy that is gravitationally bound to the Andromeda Galaxy.

The Moon never gets this close to the Andromeda Galaxy in the sky! However, as you can see, the Andromeda Galaxy spans a greater area of the sky than the Moon. In fact, many celestial objects pictured in this book are "bigger" than the Moon in the sky, but can't be seen to their fullest extent with our eyes because they are very faint.

Galaxies

T he debate over the true nature of galaxies was concluded at the end of 1924, after Edwin Hubble had photographed galaxies with the new 100-inch diameter telescope. He had conclusive proof that they were islands of stars. This ushered in a new age for astronomy.

A Universe filled with different types of galaxies

There are about 125 billion galaxies that contain all the stars in the Universe. There are no stars between galaxies. The stars in galaxies are gravitationally bound and revolve around a concentrations of stars at their centers. After taking thousands of photographs of galaxies, astronomers discovered that there are three basic shapes.

The most common type of galaxy is the **elliptical**. The smallest and largest galaxies are elliptical. These resemble balls or elongated balls. Overall, the stars in ellipticals are smaller and older than the stars in our sky. Inside these galaxies, there is little gas and dust to form new stars.

A second type of galaxy is the **spiral**, which resembles its name. The galaxy that we live in, the Milky Way Galaxy, is a spiral. Spirals look flatter, like dishes. They have round bulging centers out of which curved arms radiate. Spirals often have lots of gas and dust in their arms from which new stars are born. Although spiral galaxies account for only a small percentage of galaxies, their arms and centers are bright, so they stand out more than the others.

Finally, there are two kinds of **irregular** galaxies. One kind appears to be the result of the collision of galaxies. The other is usually a smaller galaxy being distorted or pulled on by the gravity of a nearby larger galaxy. In both cases, these galaxies have mixed up insides, often with no centers or nuclei and containing large amounts of gas and dust, out of which new stars can form. The Large and Small Magellanic Clouds (see page 11), visible from the southern hemisphere, are two close irregular galaxies that are being distorted by the gravitational pull of our galaxy.

Moving fast

After Hubble determined the true nature of galaxies in 1924, he wanted to know their distances. In 1929, he made another important discovery. He found that the farther away a galaxy was, the faster it was moving away. He and other astronomers then confirmed that *all* distant galaxies were moving away, as if from an explosion. Eventually, this information helped provide evidence for the idea of the "Big Bang."

CONTINUED ON NEXT PAGE

At least eighty percent (80%) of all galaxies are of the **elliptical** type. These galaxies are spherical in shape, that is, they resemble a ball, or elongated ball similar to a short watermelon. They lack arms and are composed mostly of older stars, which revolve about their centers "every which way," much like a swarm of bees. Pictured is a large elliptical (designated M87) found in the direction of the spring constellation Virgo. It is 55 million light years away and has a diameter of 133,000 light years. This galaxy is visible with a small telescope.

At most ten percent (10%) of all galaxies are classified as **spiral**. These galaxies are dish shaped. They have a central bulge, out of which curved arms radiate. In spirals, many stars are born in the arms where huge hydrogen clouds exist. Pictured is the Whirlpool Galaxy (designated M51), located in the direction of the constellation Ursa Major (the Big Dipper is part of this constellation). It is 15 million light years away and has a diameter of 35,000 light years. It can be seen in a small telescope, but requires dark skies. The smaller galaxy on the left is much farther away than the Whirlpool.

Galaxies

The remaining ten percent (10%) of galaxies are classified as **irregular** because they look lumpy or irregular in shape. Astronomers believe that some irregulars represent two or more galaxies that have collided, while others might result from being gravitationally distorted by nearby larger galaxies. Pictured is an irregular galaxy seen in the direction of the constellation Ursa Major (designated M82 and near the Big Dipper) which is visible with a small telescope, even in cities with lots of light pollutions. It is 17 million light years away, has a diameter of 55,000 light years and probably is the result of two galaxies that collided.

The above galaxy, known as the Sombrero Galaxy (named for its resemblance to the sombrero hat), was once thought to be an elliptical galaxy. Today, it has been reclassified as a spiral galaxy. Astronomers, like other scientists reevaluate and update information and ideas as they learn more about the objects they study. The Sombrero Galaxy (designated M104) is located in the constellation Virgo and is visible during the summer with a small telescope. It is 65 million light years away and has a diameter of 165,000 light years.

Red shift

Something happens to the light from distant receding galaxies. The lines in the spectrums of their light (see caption at the bottom of page 28) shift or move towards the red part. The amount of the shift indicates how fast a galaxy is moving away and even provides a clue to its distance. Spectrums can also shift towards the blue part, which indicates movement towards us. Both of these phenomena are the same effect as the change in pitch heard when a train approaches and moves away. This shifting of the spectrum has proved immensely helpful in determining the movement or speed of most celestial objects.

Bumping into one another

For their size, galaxies are millions of times closer to one another than the stars they contain. For example, our Milky Way Galaxy and the Andromeda Galaxy are only 20 diameters apart from one another. On the other hand, our Sun and the closest star, Proxima Centauri, which is in the constellation Centaurus, are 29 million times farther away from one another. Proportionately, there are truly enormous amounts of space between stars, but not between galaxies.

Galaxies cluster in groups. These groups are gravitationally bound and the galaxies within them revolve around one another, but not in the orderly fashion of the planets in our solar system. The closeness of galaxies in clusters, combined with their disorderly revolutions, makes galactic collisions occur often. There is evidence to show that the Milky Way and Andromeda galaxies may collide some day.

Beginning to end

It appears that many elliptical and spiral galaxies have supermassive black holes at their very centers (you can read more about this on page 25). Astronomers are not sure if galaxies formed around black holes created at the beginning of the Universe or if the central black holes were later formed by the galaxies. In either case, this leads us to the evolution of galaxies. Galaxies are clumps of stars. Shortly after the Big Bang, billions of large clouds became the stars of galaxies. Astronomers think that elliptical galaxies may be the result of spiral galaxies colliding with one another. When they look deep into space, which is the same as looking back into time, they find that spiral galaxies were smaller and more numerous than they are now. Since galaxies frequently collide, it is a reasonable conclusion to say that the collision of 2 or 3 spirals produces an elliptical galaxy. Like anything that is not known for certain in science, this idea will be studied more.

Galaxy Facts

Number of galaxies in the Universe: Around 125 billion.

Types of galaxies: 80% are elliptical, 10% are spiral and 10% are irregular.

Diameter of galaxies: 400 to 500,000 light years.

Number of stars in a galaxy: Averages in the billions but varies from 10 million to a trillion.

Objects at the very centers of galaxies: A supermassive black hole may reside at the center of almost every galaxy.

Galaxy clusters: Galaxies cluster together in groups of a dozen to a few thousand. Clusters of galaxies form strands that stretch across the Universe.

Distance between galaxies: Around 500,000 light years or less for those in a cluster.

Stuff between galaxies: Traces of hydrogen, helium, carbon, nitrogen and oxygen molecules.

Objects inside galaxies: Stars, binary stars, nebulae, white dwarfs, neutron stars, black holes. Supernovae explosions occur in galaxies. Globular clusters surround galaxies.

Spiral galaxy in the constellation Ursa Major (designated M101) which can be found in the area of the Big Dipper. This galaxy is almost 18 million light years away and has a diameter of 147,000 light years.

Unfortunately, none of the objects shown in this book look as big, bright and colorful through a telescope as they do in the pictures. Through most telescopes, these objects appear smaller, fainter and whitish. Why? Simply because all of these objects are faint and our eyes cannot detect colors at very low light levels. Nor can our eyes accumulate light like photographic film or digital cameras. Don't let this dissuade you from looking at these objects through a telescope or binoculars. There is nothing like seeing them yourself and views through these instruments, especially those of star clusters, are often better than photographs!

Our Milky Way Galaxy

Our Milky Way Galaxy is just one of about 125 billion galaxies in the Universe. Our Sun is just one of about 100 billion stars in our galaxy.

Name

The Ancients unknowingly named our galaxy. When they looked up into the night sky, they saw a faint irregular path that stretched across it and called this the Milky Way. They did not know that it represented the faint glow from the bulk of the stars in our galaxy. When astronomers discovered this fact, they continued to use the name that our galaxy had been called for centuries.

Shape

Our galaxy is a spiral and it is bigger than most galaxies. Astronomers are not certain why some galaxies have elliptical shapes and

Our Milky Way Galaxy may look like this spiral galaxy located in the constellation Eridanus (to the right of Orion). This galaxy is 50 million light years away and has a diameter of 100,000 light years, which makes it about the same size as ours. This galaxy is not visible with a small telescope.

others look like spirals, but they think that ellipticals result from the collision of spirals. In our galaxy, the oldest stars are near the core, while the arms contain the youngest. All spiral galaxies have differences. Our nucleus is more elongated than some. Astronomers call this type a "barred center." Major arms start on opposite sides of the bar.

Center

The core or nucleus of our galaxy contains most of the stars and it is about 30,000 light years away in the direction of the constellation Sagittarius. Astronomers have discovered that a supermassive black hole exists there, with a mass of about 2.5 million suns.

Shaped like a flat dish. This edge-on, false-colored picture of our galaxy was obtained by taking infrared images (see The Electromagnetic Spectrum on page 26) of the Milky Way Band that stretches across the night sky. Infrared imagery allows astronomers to get past the gas and dust that blocks much of our view. The black and white picture to the right shows some of the nebulae and dust surrounding the bulging core, or nucleus, of our galaxy. This bulge is 10,000 light years wide and 6,500 light years in height.

Arms

If we could view our entire galaxy like we can view the Andromeda Galaxy, we would see four distinct arms curving outward from the core. Also, we would notice that there are shorter branches and knots here and there. Our Sun is closer to the edge of our galaxy in what astronomers call the Orion-Cygnus arm. Farther out from us is an arm called the Perseus arm and closer in is the Sagittarius arm. These arms are in the direction of the constellations with those names.

The Small Magellanic Cloud (SMC) as it appears from the southern hemisphere. Although this irregular galaxy is 195,000 light years away, it is gravitationally bound and being pulled on by our Milky Way Galaxy. The SMC is about 10,000 light years in length and has a mass about 20 billion times that of our Sun.

Our Milky Way Galaxy

Type of galaxy: Spiral galaxy with a slightly straight or "barred" center.

Diameter: 75,000 to 100,000 light years.

Center: Our Sun is about 30,000 light years from the center. The center of our galaxy is in the direction of the constellation Sagittarius, visible during the summer.

Total mass: About 1 trillion times the mass of our Sun.

Number of stars: About 100 billion.

Revolution of our Sun around our galaxy's center: About 220 million years.

Closest companion galaxies: The Large and Small Magellanic Clouds which are visible to the naked eye from the southern hemisphere.

Local Group: Our galaxy is one of 3 dozen in a small cluster called the Local Group.

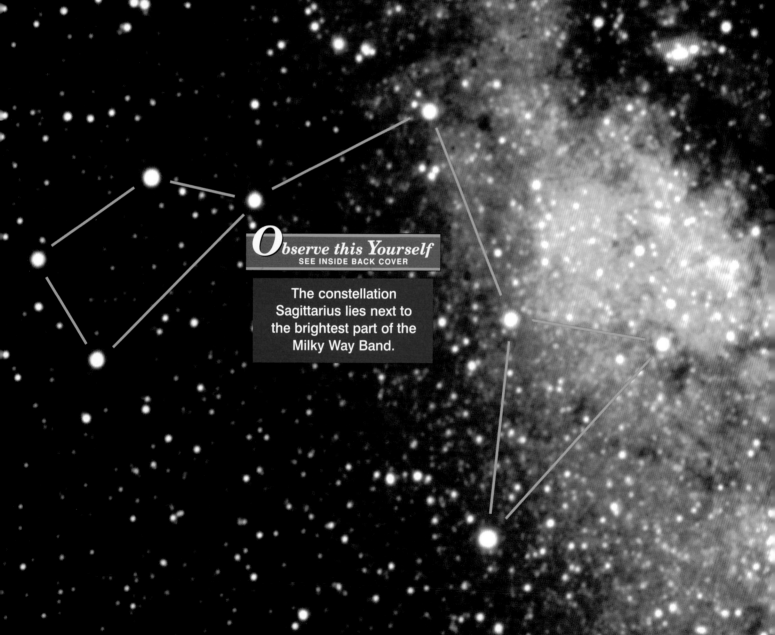

The heart of the Milky Way, that is, the direction toward the center of our Milky Way Galaxy, is between the constellations Sagittarius and Scorpius. This area of the Milky Way Band is also the widest and brightest. Although it is visible just above the southern horizon from July to September, city lights and pollution can easily wash it out so that it cannot be seen.

*O*bserve this *Yourself*
SEE INSIDE BACK COVER

The constellation Sagittarius lies next to the brightest part of the Milky Way Band.

The Milky Way Band

Astronomers estimate that there are about 100 billion stars in our galaxy. However, we can only see about 5,000 of them with our eyes. Where are the rest? Most of them make up the Milky Way Band and are too far away to be seen individually.

Why we can't see our galaxy

It's hard to see the outside of something when you are inside it! When you are inside your home, you can't see the outside, but you do see some of the house. The same idea applies to our Milky Way Galaxy — we can only see some of it because we are inside it. Often, people ask why we can't send a spacecraft out to take a picture. Well, the spacecraft would have to travel for billions of years to get far enough away to take a picture of our whole galaxy.

Inside out

The view we have of our galaxy is from where we are — the inside. Since our galaxy is a spiral, most of its stars are spread across a flat dish. So, by looking outward from where we are, all we see is a circular band of mostly faint, far-away stars. To get a similar effect, place your head inside a hula-hoop and look around.

The Band

The Milky Way Band looks like an irregular whitish path that circles the skies of the northern and southern hemispheres. It is irregular in shape because the stars in our galaxy are not evenly distributed. On any given night, we see about half of the Band. All the stars that we do see in the night sky are the very closest. However, the billions of stars that make up the band are so far away that they appear only as a faint glow. Although astronomers can see many of the Milky Way Band stars with telescopes, they cannot see all the stars in our galaxy because our views are often blocked by gas and dust in the arms and many branches.

Ancient beliefs

Everything in the night sky was a mystery to ancient civilizations. Their knowledge of nature was very elementary because they did not have the instruments to study it like we do today. And much of their belief systems were wrapped up in their religions, which we now look upon as myths and legends. For many of these civilizations, the Milky Way Band was considered the River of Heaven and was thought of as the road that departed souls took to reach their final resting place. Some Native Americans also believed that the bright stars in the Milky Way Band were campfires where departed souls camped and rested. One of the earliest references to the Band being milky was in a hymn written around 800 BC by the ancient Greek writer Homer.

+ **This cross marks the direction toward the center of our Milky Way Galaxy.**

Try This

A part of the Milky Way Band is usually visible in the night sky.

1. The Milky Way Band stands out best in country skies, away from city lights. You only need your eyes to see it — best from July through March.

2. The brightest and thickest part (same as that shown in this picture) comes up from the southern horizon during July and through September. This is a spectacular sight!

3. Use a telescope or binoculars to observe the Milky Way Band and then an area away from it. Notice the difference in the number of stars?

Inside Galaxies The Birth of Stars

Stars are born inside giant clouds called nebulae (the singular is nebula) that are composed mostly of hydrogen and some helium gas molecules. There is an abundance of nebulae in the arms of our galaxy. This is where most new stars are born.

Out of clouds

Nebulae can easily span 150 light years. These clouds are large and "thin." They would be considered vacuums on Earth because they contain as few as 1,600 atoms per cubic inch. However, even though these clouds are thin, concentration can happen inside, just like raindrops condense out of clouds. Astronomers have identified several ways that gas can be pushed and concentrated in an area. The simplest concentration happens when clouds collide. For example, the gas thrown from a supernova explosion can ram into clouds. Also, nearby starlight can push on the clouds (yes, sunlight or starlight can push and move molecules in space). When concentrations do occur, they can have diameters 300 or more times than that of our solar system. Concentrations are large and massive, so they have gravity. Gravity slowly takes over and further condenses the concentration. By this time, the concentration is rotating (most objects in the Universe have some spin) and heating up as it further contracts. Because the concentration rotates, its shape starts to flatten out and can resemble a donut with a bulging center.

Ignition

This whole concentration is often referred to as a cocoon and inside, around the center, is the protostar. The cocoon is opaque from dust. The protostar becomes a star when the temperature and pressure at its core become so great that sustained nuclear fusion takes place. Nuclear fusion is the process of forcing or "fusing" four hydrogen atoms together to produce one helium atom. This process releases an enormous amount of energy as a very small amount of matter gets converted to energy according to Einstein's famous equation $E=mc^2$. Four hydrogen atoms weigh about 1% more than one helium atom. It is this one percent of extra matter that gets converted to pure energy.

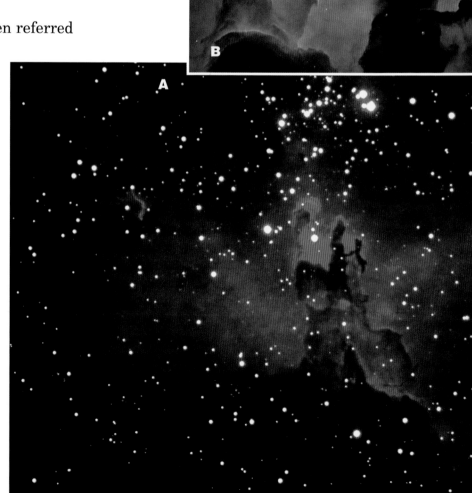

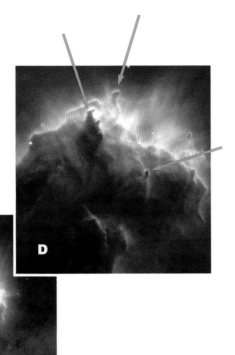

When the new star becomes hot enough, it reveals itself by pushing away leftover gas and dust in the cocoon. Astronomers can see newborn stars within their opaque cocoons by using telescopes with instrumentation that can detect infrared radiation. See the "hot pot" example described on page 26.

Double and more

About half of all stars are part of a multiple star system where two or more stars revolve around one another. Many binary stars can be viewed with a small telescope. Castor, in the constellation Gemini, is a favorite (see back inside cover).

Solar systems

Since 1987, astronomers have found other planets orbiting stars. Planets condense out of the protostar disks along with the new stars. Planets, like the Earth, are made of rocks and metal, material that was just dust in the protostar disks.

This stellar nursery (pictures A – D), called the Eagle Nebula, is located in the constellation Serpens and is visible with a small telescope during the summer. See the back inside cover for its location. This nebula is about 9,000 light years away and its longest dimension, the span of its wings, spreads over 300 light years.

A. The entire Eagle Nebula as photographed by an Earth-based telescope from one of the observatories located on Kitt Peak, near Tucson, Arizona. Some nebulae, like this one, are named after their shape. Where are the eagle's wings and head?

B. This famous picture was taken by the *Hubble Space Telescope*, which orbits 375 miles above the Earth. This is often referred to as the "Pillars of Creation," because stars are being born inside the pillars or columns. The *Hubble Space Telescope* can capture greater detail than Earth-based telescopes because it is above our turbulent atmosphere. Can you identify where the pillars are in the bottom picture?

C & D. Enlargements of the top left pillar. Astronomers have identified protostars, which are cocoon-type concentrations of hydrogen gas inside the tops of many smaller columns or fingers. The arrows point to three fingers. The cocoon concentrations are hidden by the dust but are visible in infrared (see The Electromagnetic Spectrum starting on page 26). The width of these fingers is about one-quarter of a light year. Remember, our solar system has a diameter of just 11 light *hours*. The closest star to the Sun is just over 4 light *years* away.

The easiest stellar nursery to find and observe is the Great Orion Nebula located below the belt of the constellation Orion. It is very spectacular even in small telescopes. This nebula is lit by four stars, called the Trapezium, born about one million years ago. They are also visible in a small telescope and are located in the brightest, that is, the white part of the nebula. Astronomers have found evidence of other stars forming in this nebula, which is 1,500 light years away and 39 light years across.

Nebulae

The Horsehead Nebula in the constellation Orion requires a large telescope to be seen. It is located just below Orion's left belt star. This nebula is actually a "dark nebula" that is in front of a lit one. It is dark because there are no nearby stars to light it up. The Horsehead is 1,500 light years away and 2.5 light years in height.

Nebulae are often called molecular clouds because they contain molecules of hydrogen, helium and other elements. They vary in size and shape but can span distances of several to hundreds of light years. Today, most nebulae are found in the arms of spiral galaxies. Some represent recycled material from stars that have died. Shortly after the Big Bang, there were enormous nebulae out of which formed the innumerable stars of galaxies.

All nebulae are basically the same, but they are lit differently. Nebulae that are not near any stars appear dark or black. We see these as silhouettes when they are in front of stars or other bright nebulae. The Horsehead Nebula, pictured to the left, is a good example of this type. Other nebulae glow in a fashion similar to neon signs. The hydrogen in these emission nebulae are excited to fluoresce a pinkish color by the highly energetic ultraviolet light of some nearby stars. A third type of nebula is dimly lit by reflecting light from nearby stars. These reflection nebulae appear bluish in color from scattering light, which is the same process that makes our daytime sky blue.

The Omega Nebula (designated M17), which lies north of the constellation Sagittarius, is very easy to see in a small telescope. It is 4,900 light years away and stretches across 57 light years. Its reddish color is produced by highly energetic light from nearby stars exciting the hydrogen atoms to fluoresce, which is similar to the way that neon signs light up. The red color cannot be seen by your eyes when viewing through a telescope.

Observe this Yourself
SEE INSIDE BACK COVER

Observe this Yourself
SEE INSIDE BACK COVER

Inside Galaxies Star Clusters

Stars are born in groups or clusters. It would be rare for just one star to be born from a nebula. Hundreds of clusters can easily be observed with a small telescope.

Open clusters

An open cluster is a group of stars born together from the same nebula. The number of stars varies from a dozen to a thousand or so. The best-known open cluster is the Pleiades or Seven Sisters, pictured below. Often, open clusters slowly spread and break apart because their stars move away from one another. Our Sun was born in a group that has broken up.

Globular clusters

Globular clusters are a distinct type of star cluster. They resemble cotton balls and contain anywhere from 100,000 to a million stars. Overall, the stars in globulars are much older than those in open clusters. Our Milky Way Galaxy has about 200 globular clusters that surround its nucleus in a ball-like halo. Globular clusters are easy to see in small telescopes, but they are spectacular in 12-inch or larger diameter telescopes!

Observe this Yourself
SEE INSIDE BACK COVER

A beautiful cluster of stars near the constellation Scorpius, visible during the summer with binoculars. Remember, a cluster of stars represents stars born together from the same nebula. This cluster (designated M7) contains about 80 stars that are 200 million years old, 780 light years away and span an area of 18 light years.

The Pleiades or Seven Sisters (designated M45) is a cluster that is located in the constellation Taurus and is visible during the winter with the naked eyes. However, the nebulosity around it, which is lit by reflected light from the stars, is more difficult to see. This cluster, which looks beautiful in binoculars, contains about 100 stars that are 407 light years away and span across 14 light years. These stars are about 70 million years old.

In Greek mythology, the Seven Sisters were the daughters of Atlas and Pleione. They were changed into doves and sent to the heavens as stars to avoid the romantic interests of Orion. The Pleiades rise before Orion, forever escaping him.

This large globular cluster (designated M22), is in the constellation Sagittarius and is visible in a small telescope. Globular clusters look similar to elliptical galaxies but they are not the same. This cluster is 10,000 light years away and spans 96 light years. It consists of about 100,000 stars.

Observe this Yourself
SEE INSIDE BACK COVER

Inside Galaxies Stars

T he Universe contains stars. There are more stars than anything else in the Universe. Yes, there are galaxies and nebulae, but galaxies contain stars and nebulae produce more stars. Stars are the one thing that naturally forms in the Universe.

Shining brightly

The light from stars is produced from nuclear **fusion** occurring at their centers. The first atomic bombs used nuclear **fission**, that is, they broke atoms apart to create their destructive energy. Today, atomic bombs produce their energy from nuclear fusion. Although this is the same process that fuels stars, the Sun and stars do it naturally.

Fusion occurs at the centers of stars where the pressure and heat are so great, they force four hydrogen atoms to combine and form one helium atom. Four hydrogen atoms weigh slightly more than one helium atom. In fact, they weigh about one percent more. That one percent of matter gets converted into pure energy — the light that we see from our Sun and stars.

Normal size, mass, brightness, temperature and life

Stars come in all sizes, but even the smallest are large and massive. Our Sun is an average-sized star. It has a diameter of 865,000 miles. The diameter of normal-sized stars varies from about 1/3 to 10 times the diameter of our Sun. Mass, the amount of matter that a star contains, varies from 1/10 to 40 times that of our Sun. Brightness varies from 1/100 to over 1,000,000 times that of our Sun and the smallest stars have surface temperatures of just

5,000°F while the largest reach 70,000°F. Our Sun will last about 10 billion years, while the smallest stars may last a trillion and the largest only a million.

This information applies to normal stars. There are stars that are much smaller or much larger than mentioned above, but they represent special cases of stars at the end of their lives. This includes stars known as white dwarfs, neutron stars, black holes, giants and supergiants.

"Yardstick" stars

Cepheid variables are famous stars because they gave astronomers the "yardstick" tool, that is, the means for measuring the distances to stars within our galaxy and even nearby galaxies (but not distant ones).

Variable stars change in brightness, taking a few days to a year or more. Cepheid variables are named after one of the first of this kind observed in the constellation Cepheus, which is visible in the northern sky. These types of variables are either giant or supergiant stars near the end of their lives. They slowly change in brightness over a period of a few days to months by expanding and contracting in size. Their diameters change anywhere from 5 to 10 percent. Polaris, the North Star, is a Cepheid variable but the amount that it changes in brightness is very small. In 1912, Henrietta Leavitt discovered that the actual brightness of a Cepheid variable depends on the period of its pulsation. Other astronomers then used this information to measure the distances to Cepheid variables throughout our galaxy and

Observe this Yourself
SEE INSIDE BACK COVER

The star Betelgeuse in the constellation of Orion. This is one of the few images of a star other than our Sun and was taken by the orbiting *Hubble Space Telescope*. This supergiant star has a diameter of almost a billion miles.

The color of a star depends on its surface temperature. Hotter stars appear blue or white, while cooler stars are red. There are no green stars because green is in the middle of the spectrum and gets washed out.

beyond. By comparing the brightness of Cepheid variable stars observed from Earth to their actual brightness, astronomers calculate their distance from us.

All the elements

When the Universe formed, there were only two elements, hydrogen and helium. All the other elements of the periodic table were produced by stars. This includes metals and silicates, which make up rocks. Our Sun is a second generation star. It and the planets contain elements created from stars that have lived and died. Some of the elements that make up the Earth were formed by very large stars that ended their lives in supernova explosions.

Giants and supergiants

Really large stars are "puffed up" stars near the end of their lives. Our Sun, near the end of its life, will expand to about the size of Mercury's orbit. Stars that are much more massive than our Sun become supergiants. Their outer atmospheres can expand to at least 1,500 times the diameter of our Sun. The outer atmosphere of the supergiant Betelgeuse in the constellation Orion would almost reach the orbit of Jupiter. On the next pages, you will find out more about the fate of these stars.

Star Facts

Our Sun: Our Sun is a typical or average star. It has a diameter of 865,000 miles and is yellowish in color. It has a mass 333,000 times that of Earth and is about 4.5 billion years old.

Mass of stars: The mass or amount of matter in stars varies from just 1/10 to over 40 times the mass of our Sun.

Normal Sizes: Diameters vary from 1/3 to over 10 times the diameter of our Sun.

Composition: The composition of a normal star is 75 percent hydrogen gas and 25 percent helium gas, including traces of other elements.

Life span of stars: The smallest may last a trillion years or more while the largest may last only a million years. Our Sun will have a total life of about 10 billion years.

A Red Supergiant

This very small yellow dot represents the size of our Sun compared to this red supergiant which has a diameter 1,000 times larger. This makes it slightly smaller than Antares, the brightest star in the constellation Scorpius (visible during the summer). A red supergiant is a "puffed up" star in a final stage of its life before it explodes as a supernova.

The length of this white line represents the distance from the Earth to the Sun, which is 93 million miles.

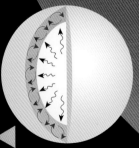

Stars like our Sun create energy at their centers from nuclear fusion, which transforms hydrogen into helium. The energy radiates from the center and then gets circulated near the surface.

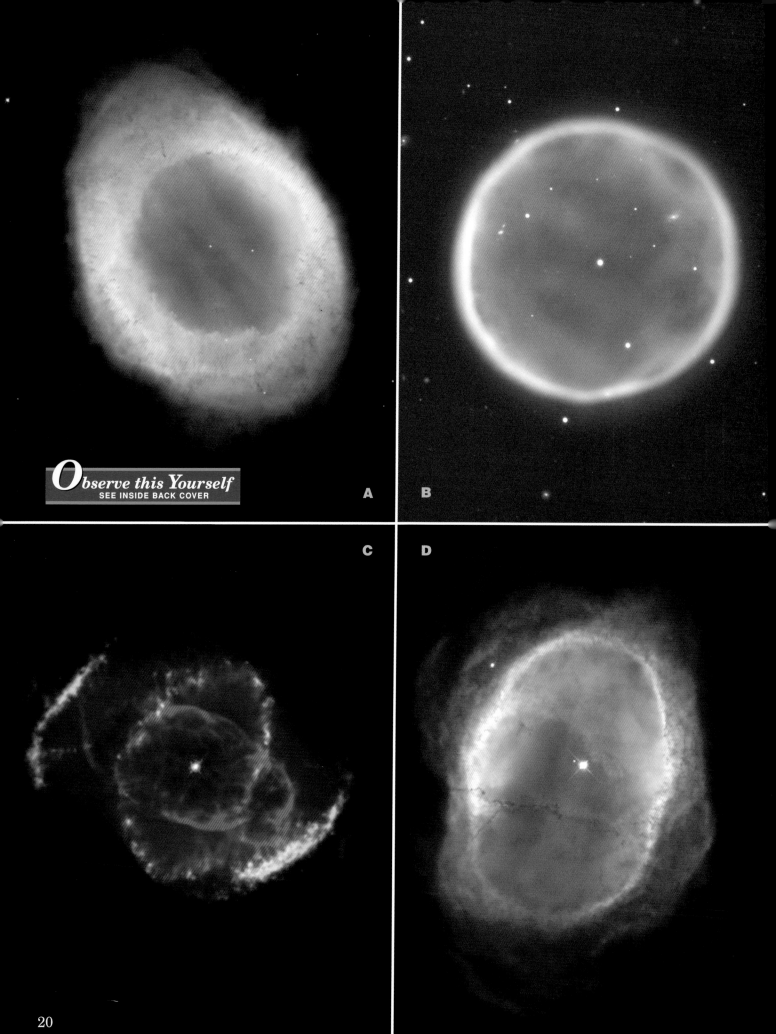

A

B

C

D

Inside Galaxies Dying Stars

Stars live long lives. But eventually, stars die because they run out of fuel for nuclear fusion.

The smallest live longest

The smallest "normal" stars, which have masses about 1/10 that of our Sun live long lives. These stars are called red dwarfs because they are small in diameter and red in color. They slowly and efficiently fuse hydrogen into helium for a trillion or more years. Red dwarfs die quietly and become cold dark cinders.

Stars the size of our Sun

Medium-sized stars about the size of our Sun end their lives differently. These stars burn hotter and faster than the smallest stars, so their average life span is about 10 billion years. Towards the end of their lives, after fusing much of their hydrogen into helium, they end up with a core that

A. The Ring Nebula (designated M57), located in the constellation Lyra, is visible during the summer months. This is a favorite object and can be seen with a small telescope. It is 1,140 light years away and less than one-half a light year in length, which makes it 335 times larger than the diameter of our solar system.

B. This pretty blue planetary nebula is in the constellation Hercules. It is 7,000 light years away and has a diameter of 5 light years.

C. The Cat's Eye Nebula in the constellation Draco is estimated to be just 1,000 years old.

D. The Southern Ring Nebula, located in the constellation Vela, is 2,000 light years away and has a diameter of about half a light year, which is the same size as the Ring Nebula in Lyra.

The Hourglass Nebula, in the southern hemisphere constellation Musca, is a favorite and is often referred to as "The Eye of God." It is 8,000 light years away and has a length of three-fourths of a light year.

The Owl Nebula (designated M97) is located along the bottom of the bowl of the Big Dipper. It is 1,600 light years away and has a large diameter of 79 light years, which indicates that it may be an older planetary nebula.

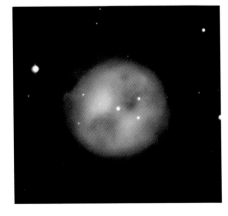

is mostly helium, but is surrounded by an outer shell or atmosphere of hydrogen. There comes a point when the helium core starts to collapse, which causes it to heat up tremendously. This extra heat causes the outer hydrogen atmosphere to start fusing into helium, which makes it expand enormously — to diameters as large as the Earth's orbit. These stars become giant stars.

Giant stars, planetary nebulae and white dwarfs

The thin outer atmospheres of giant stars are eventually pushed farther and farther out into space to form what are called planetary nebulae. Planetary nebulae have nothing to do with planets! This is an old name given to them before anyone understood their true nature. The word planet was used because many are roundish, resembling, to a degree, planets. Planetary nebulae are not always round. Their shape can be affected by magnetic fields generated by the dying star.

Planetary nebulae can expand to 3 light years or more in size and eventually dissipate, perhaps lasting for 10,000 years. Their shedded hydrogen gas shells often give off their own light, stimulated by the energetic ultraviolet light emitted by the collapsed star, now known as a white dwarf.

White dwarfs represent the final remnants of stars like our Sun. They are very dense, with very hot surfaces exceeding 45,000° F, which is hot enough to produce the energetic light that pushes the gas around them outward. White dwarfs are about the same size as the Earth.

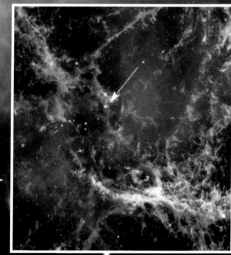

The Crab Nebula (designated M1) in the constellation Taurus was created from a supernova explosion that occurred on July 4th, 1054. It is 6,500 light years away and stretches across 11 light years. What remained of the exploding star became a rapidly rotating neutron star known as a pulsar (that spins on its axis 30 times a second) with a diameter of about 10 miles. To the right is a closeup of the Crab's center with the arrow pointing to the neutron star.

Supernova Deaths

T he last supernova explosion of a star in our galaxy occurred in 1604. The light produced from these explosions is anywhere from 600 million to 4 billion times the brightness of our Sun. They remain bright for several months and then fade over the course of a year. These explosions are rare events that produce more light than an entire galaxy. To study them, astronomers scan galaxies looking for these awesome beacons.

Two types

There are two types of supernova explosions. The fainter type is produced when a massive star uses up its nuclear fuel. When this happens, the huge core collapses suddenly, sending out a shock wave that blasts the remaining atmosphere outward. The brightest type occurs in a binary star system where a white dwarf gravitationally pulls in so much material from the other star that it causes the white dwarf to further collapse, fueling uncontrolled nuclear fusion to produce the most violent type of explosion in the Universe.

Neutron stars, pulsars and black holes

Supernovae can create neutron stars or black holes depending on how much material or mass is left after the explosion. A neutron star is an object about 10 miles in diameter and a sugar cube of its material weighs 100 million tons. Pulsars are rapidly rotating neutron stars, rotating up to 1,000 times per second. See the next page for more information on black holes.

Novae

At one time, astronomers thought that novae might be baby supernovae. Well, after collecting and analyzing data on novae, they discovered that they are quite different. A nova is like a repeating camera "flash." Nova flashes occur in binary systems, where two stars are orbiting close to one another. One of the stars is normal and the other is a white dwarf. The stars are close enough that the outer atmosphere of the normal star gets pulled onto the surface of the white dwarf. When a substantial amount of the hydrogen atmosphere has accumulated on the white dwarf's surface, it ignites like a nuclear fusion bomb. Afterward, the white dwarf remains intact and the process begins all over again. These flashes are 100,000 times brighter than our Sun.

A supernova explosion that happened in 1987 but was visible only from the southern hemisphere. The star that exploded was not in our galaxy, but located in the Large Magellanic Cloud (see page 11).

Remnant of gas from a supernova explosion, known as the Veil Nebula situated in the constellation Cygnus. This explosion occurred about 20,000 years ago and the gas arc is part of a loose loop that stretches over 5.5 Moon diameters in the sky.

A "jet" created by a supermassive black hole at the center of an elliptical galaxy (designated M87) that can be found in the direction of the constellation Virgo. This large galaxy is 55 million light years away. Black holes can shoot off jets of electrons from matter circling inward.

Quasars are young, very distant galaxies with highly active supermassive black holes at their centers. These galaxies are so bright that they appear starlike, instead of fuzzy like normal galaxies. The high energy is created from surrounding gas swirling inward to the black hole, heating to millions of degrees, giving off light and other electromagnetic radiation.

These are actual photos taken by the *Hubble Space Telescope* of a galaxy's center, in the direction of the constellation Virgo. The lighted glowing area in the center photo is about 1,000 light years across. The reddish loop is gas being ejected. The gas surrounding this supermassive black hole slowly circles inward and forms a donut shape called an accretion disk. The gas from this disk eventually crosses into the event horizon.

Inside Galaxies Black Holes

T he most mysterious objects in the Universe may conjure up thoughts of devouring monsters, but black holes are nothing more than fairly tame dead stars.

What exactly is a black hole?

The idea of a black hole came shortly after Isaac Newton developed his equation about gravity in 1687. A black hole is a celestial object with so much gravity that not even light can escape from its surface. Celestial black holes are very massive, that is, very dense objects made of lots of matter packed into a tiny ball.

Small to large

Black holes come in a variety of sizes, from small to supermassive. A small black hole has a mass at least three times that of our Sun. Supermassive black holes are believed to reside at the center of most, if not all galaxies. These black holes are estimated to have masses millions of times that of our Sun.

Becoming a black hole

Small black holes form from the remains of supernova explosions. If the mass that remains after these explosions is three or more times that of our Sun, the object will automatically collapse to become a black hole. Anything less masssve than three solar masses will become a neutron star or white dwarf. Our Sun does not have enough mass to become a black hole — it will become a white dwarf. Small black holes can only be created from stars much more massive than our Sun.

Supermassive black holes, located at the center of galaxies, may become more massive by pulling in extra matter when galaxies collide.

If this watch were thrown into a black hole, it would seem to take forever to disappear into the abyss. Also, as it got closer, the watch would be stretched and squeezed by the huge difference in gravitational pull between short distances.

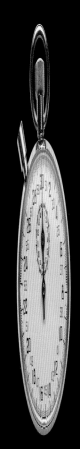

Zero in size?

According to the mathematics, all black holes, no matter how massive, have zero diameters. This seems difficult to believe, so scientists are studying this idea further to see if black holes might just have very small diameters. But astronomers are pretty sure of one thing: the smallest black holes, those having just three times the mass of our Sun, would have diameters smaller than the periods printed on these pages.

Event horizons

Although black holes may only be the size of a period at the end of a sentence, they create around them a larger area of no return called an event horizon. If you enter the event horizon, you cannot escape from the black hole. The diameter of the event horizon gets larger as the black hole gets more massive. A black hole with the mass of three of our Suns has an event horizon 11 miles in diameter, whereas a million solar-mass black hole has a diameter of 5,600,000 miles, which is 14 times smaller than Mercury's orbit around the Sun.

Black holes are not vacuum cleaners

If our Sun suddenly became a black hole, the planets would continue to orbit the black hole just like they did the Sun. A black hole does not act like a vacuum cleaner and suck things into it! A spacecraft could safely visit a black hole by orbiting around it. But, if something gets too close to a black hole (actually, the event horizon), it will get pulled in. However, this is no different than a spacecraft crashing into a planet if it comes too close to it without entering an orbit.

The Electromagnetic

What is the electromagnetic spectrum and why is it so important to astronomers? There is a lot more to the Universe than what we see with our eyes. Astronomers study electromagnetic radiation in the Universe so they can better understand the "whole" cosmos.

Matter and radiation energy

The Universe is made of matter and radiation energy. Matter is anything composed of atoms. Our bodies and all the things around us are made of matter. Radiation energy is different. It has effects on matter, but it is not made of atoms. For example, radio waves, microwaves and light are radiation energies that have effects on matter and our everyday world. We generate radio waves to communicate on phones. We use microwaves to heat food, and the light from the Sun warms our planet. Matter is made of particles that have weight. Radiation energy is not made of matter; it is energy and has no weight.

Radiation energy is not radioactivity. Often these terms are confused. Radioactivity is caused by atoms decaying and emitting (ejecting) subatomic particles.

Electromagnetic radiation, waves and particles

The word radiation means energy that takes the form of a wave or particle. So, radiation energy has two faces because it acts both like a wave and like a particle. Ripples in a pond are a good example of waves. A bullet shot from a gun would be an example of a particle or packet of energy. Remember, radiation energy is not made of atoms. The wave property of energy allows radiation to bend and come to a focus in a telescope. The particle property, which can be thought of as packets of energy, allows radiation to heat up objects or produce electricity in photoelectric cells.

Electromagnetic spectrum

The electromagnetic spectrum represents the span of all the types of radiation energy in the Universe. This spectrum, as illustrated at the bottom of this page, shows that range. Out of the entire electromagnetic spectrum, the only part that our eyes can detect is **visible light**.

Seeing and detecting what our eyes can't

A cooking pot that is hot looks the same as one at room temperature. So, without touching them, how can you tell the difference between them? The hot pot is emitting heat in the form of infrared radiation. Scientists can use special instruments to detect infrared radiation coming from hot objects.

CONTINUED ON PAGE 28

A chart of the Electromagnetic Spectrum. Although radiation has the dual property of acting like a wave and like a particle of energy, it is most often represented in its wave form. The span of electromagnetic radiation is continuous. There are no gaps in the spectrum. The names given to the various radiation types are names for a range of wavelengths. The longer waves, like radio waves, have the least amount of energy, while shorter wavelengths are more energetic.

▼

Span of Electromagnetic Radiation

R A D I O   W A V E S

Long Wave **AM Radio** **FM Radio** **TV** **Microwaves**

Radio waves in the cosmos are sometimes produced from violent stellar events taking place in galaxies.

Used for long distance telephone communication and to cook food.

The distance from one Long Wave crest to another can be miles.

The crest to crest distance of FM Radio waves start at 16 feet while AM Radio waves extend to over 3,000 feet.

TV waves average 15 feet from crest to crest.

It takes an average of 25 Microwaves to span an inch.

Spectrum

A

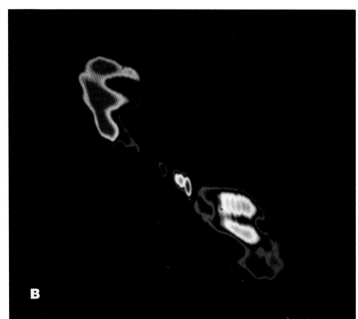

B

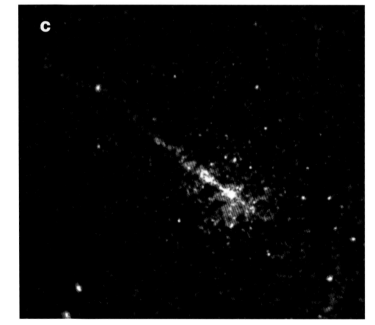

C

Three faces of the galaxy Centaurus A, the designation of the most active radio source in the constellation Centaurus. This elliptical galaxy, which has most likely collided with a spiral galaxy (the dark band), is 11 million light years away and has a diameter of 48,000 light years. If our Milky Way Galaxy were a radio galaxy, we would experience a tremendous amount of interference with our telephone, radio and TV communications. Astronomers believe that there is a supermassive black hole at the center of Centaurus A.

A. A picture of Centaurus A taken in the visible part of the electromagnetic spectrum. This is what you see with your eyes.

B. False-color radio wave image of Centaurus A. Red indicates the areas with the strongest radio signals. The upper left and lower right "lobes" extend considerably farther than the visible part of the galaxy.

C. False-color X-ray image of Centaurus A. This "line" is called a jet and was ejected by the supermassive black hole at the galaxy's center.

◀ **Longer Wavelengths**   **Shorter Wavelengths** ▶   27

Infrared	Visible Light	Ultraviolet	X rays	Gamma rays
Felt as heat from a fire or a light bulb. Visible to some insects and mammals and to humans using infrared night goggles.	The only part of the electromagnetic spectrum that human eyes can see.	Causes sunburn. Makes some rocks and insects fluoresce.	Produced from matter near black holes that gets heated to millions of degrees.	Short bursts of energy produced from supernovae explosions.
It takes an average of 200 Infrared waves to span an inch.	It take 46,200 green Light waves to span an inch.	It takes 2.5 million Ultraviolet waves to span an inch.	It takes 250 million X ray waves to span an inch.	It takes 25 billion Gamma ray waves to span an inch.

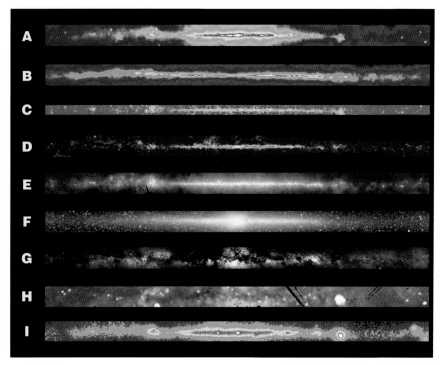

The entire Milky Way Band as it appears in different wavelengths of the electromagnetic spectrum. Special telescopes or other instruments were used to record each of these images. The colors are false color and were generated by computers to indicate signal intensity.

A. TV length **Radio Waves**

B. Long **Microwaves**

C. Medium **Microwaves**

D. Short **Microwaves**

E. Longer **Infrared**

F. Short **Infrared**. See larger picture on page 10.

G. **Visible** light waves

H. **X-ray** waves

I. **Gamma** ray waves

The visible spectrum of the star Arcturus (a very bright star in the constellation Bootes — see inside back cover). Astronomers use a special instrument called a spectrograph to spread out the light from stars (this instrument works like a prism). In doing so, they find many dark lines on the spectrum indicating different chemical elements. This picture is a series of 50 long strips stacked on top of one another. Here is a case where information about a star is visible to the eyes but is too concentrated and small for the eyes to directly detect.

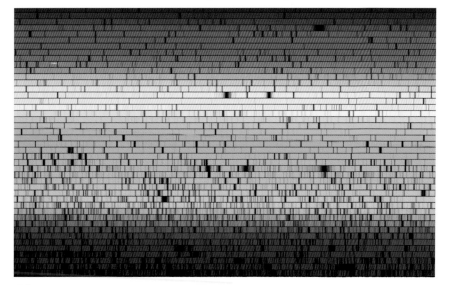

But it is not only scientists who use and can detect electromagnetic radiation. Our eyes pick up light waves to form images of the things around us. We use antennae to receive radio and television waves. Doctors use special film to record X rays. In a similar manner, astronomers use special instruments to measure and map electromagnetic radiation coming from space. Astronomers want to observe all the different types of radiation energy to get a complete picture of what is happening in the cosmos. A telescope works well for light but cannot be used to detect most other forms of electromagnetic radiation.

False colors

Since most electromagnetic radiation is invisible to our eyes, it is also colorless. To get color, scientists use computers which assign colors to the different signal intensities. Signal intensities can be thought of as the difference between bright and faint light.

Sound

The sounds that we hear with our ears are *not* electromagnetic radiation. Sound waves are produced by vibrations which can only travel through mediums like air, water or solid material. Electromagnetic radiation can travel through space or a vacuum. Sound cannot.

The speed of light

In space, all electromagnetic radiation travels at the speed of light, which is 186,282 miles per second (299,792 kilometers per second). This is the maximum speed in the Universe — nothing travels faster.

Cosmic rays

At one time, scientists had misidentified Cosmic rays as electromagnetic radiation. The name has stuck, but Cosmic rays are fast-moving subatomic particles (parts of atoms) that are thought to be expelled from supernova explosions.

Seeing the Universe

The telescope was first used by Galileo in 1609 to view the heavens. The invention of this instrument helped us begin our exploration of the Universe. However, since then, many other discoveries and inventions are enabling scientists to study all the radiation (of the electromagnetic spectrum) that comes from space.

See no radiation

Why do scientists need specialized instruments to study (detect) electromagnetic radiation? Simply because most electromagnetic radiation is invisible to our eyes! Our eyes can only see light rays.

Detecting the invisible

Since ours eyes cannot see most of the electromagnetic spectrum, how do we detect or record it? For light rays, we use film or digital cameras with lenses. Radio waves and microwaves can be focused with a metal dish which produces a very small electrical voltage that is measured. Although infrared radiation or heat energy is invisible, it can be focused with a regular camera, but special film, which you can buy at some camera stores, is needed to record the images. Scientists have figured out the materials and designs needed to focus and detect ultraviolet, X-ray and gamma-ray radiations. The X-ray and gamma-ray instruments are designed differently than regular or radio telescopes.

Looking above the atmosphere

Much of the electromagnetic radiation that comes from space cannot penetrate our atmosphere and therefore cannot be detected from the ground. For this reason, astronomers have placed many instruments above our atmosphere, orbiting Earth. Most radio waves and microwaves, infrared, ultraviolet, X rays and gamma rays cannot be detected from the ground on Earth. The radiation that easily penetrates our atmosphere include visible light, some microwaves and the TV part of radio waves.

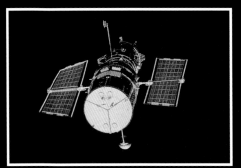

Two orbiting telescopes. *Left:* The *Hubble Space Telescope*. *Below:* The *Chandra X-ray Telescope.*

Third from top: 138-inch optical telescope near Tucson, Arizona.

Radio telescopes. *Above* is a series of 27 dishes located in New Mexico. *At left* is the famous 1,000-foot Arecibo radio dish on the island of Puerto Rico.

A Great Mystery

By 1619, Johannes Kepler, originally from Germany, had formulated three laws governing all orbiting bodies, including the planets, moons, spacecraft and binary stars. Nearly seventy years later, in 1687, Isaac Newton of England published his famous theory about gravity. Together, the orbital laws and theory of gravity gave scientists the mathematical tools to calculate the mass (see page 33 of the Glossary) of celestial objects that orbit one another. For example, by knowing the distance to the Moon and the amount of time it takes to orbit the Earth, scientists can calculate the mass of the Earth and the Moon. This is important because it allows scientists to measure mass without having to go to a planet, moon, star or galaxy.

$$F = -G\frac{Mm}{r^2}$$

Newton's Law of Gravity
This equation requires some knowledge of algebra to use. It says that F, the force of gravity between two objects, is equal to the product of their masses, M x m, divided by the square of the distance (r^2) between them. This is then multiplied by the gravitational constant G. The negative sign in front of G indicates that this is an attractive force.

The beginning of the mystery

When astronomers study the Universe, they observe and measure everything. This includes imaging all kinds of objects and measuring their distances, sizes, shapes, brightness and movements through space.

After collecting lots of information, or data, as scientists like to call it, astronomers discovered that the outer parts of galaxies revolve around their centers much faster than our calculations would predict. According to the mathematics of Kepler and Newton, galaxies should fly apart instead of staying together. This may not seem like a big deal, but after further observations, scientists can account for only about 5% of the matter in galaxies. Where or what is the other 95% that is necessary to gravitationally hold galaxies together?

What scientists do

Scientists explore and investigate, and when they don't understand or can't explain something, they search for answers. These searches often lead to new discoveries and ideas, but more importantly, they always lead to a clearer understanding of how nature works.

How do scientists do this? Most often, they carefully collect and examine evidence or scientific data. Data, meaning information or facts, can be gathered by instruments like telescopes or spacecraft. Scientists then look at all the data and try to draw conclusions based on patterns they see in it.

Is something missing?

So astronomers are trying to find "missing matter." One idea is that this matter may be "dark matter," that is, matter more like planets than bright stars. Some dark matter has been found, but there does not appear to be enough to solve the mystery.

Recently, scientists discovered that a particle of atoms called the neutrino actually has weight. Originally, they believed that this particle was more like energy and had no weight. This discovery puts more mass into galaxies, but it is still not enough to solve the mystery.

Revisiting Newton's theory of gravity

Since astronomers are still having a difficult time finding the missing matter, some scientists have proposed a new idea. They suggest that Newton's law of gravity may act very slightly differently across distances the size of galaxies. Nobody knows if this is true, but they are investigating this idea to see if it might explain the mystery.

You may discover the answer!

Scientists all over the world are studying this problem and it will take many years to solve. Some of the scientists who will help uncover the answer may be you, the readers. Individuals, like you, will become scientists to solve not only this mystery in science, but many others too. You are the future of science.

Various Ends

The Universe came into existence over 12 billion years ago from a Big Bang, but what will be its fate? Will it last forever? Most everything in nature has a beginning and end. All living creatures go through birth and death. Mountains form and erode away. Stars have births and deaths. So why should the Universe not have a end?

Expanding Universe

The Big Bang was an explosive event that popped our Universe into existence. Astronomers do not know why the Universe began in this way; it just did. Explosions cause expansion by hurling everything outward. Astronomers know that the Universe is expanding because they have been able to measure the speed and direction of galaxies' movement. In every direction they look, galaxies are fleeing away, just like from an explosion.

Density does it

Density is the weight of a substance per unit of volume. For example, a block of balsa wood weighs less than a block of aluminum, which weighs less than a block of gold. These substances take up the same amount of volume but have different weights because they have different densities. In this example, gold has the highest density. The density of the Universe may be the key to determining its final fate.

To be or not to be

If the density of the Universe may determine its fate, what could happen to it? The Universe will either continue to expand and exist forever, or will one day stop expanding and collapse back on itself. But which will happen?

If the density of the Universe is high enough, then the Universe's gravity will eventually slow its expansion to a stop, reverse its direction and finally make it collapse. This will result in all the matter and energy in the Universe coming together in what astronomers call the "Big Crunch." If the density of the Universe is too low, the Universe will continue to expand forever. In this case, the Universe does not have enough gravity to stop the expansion. The expansion continues forever with matter getting spread out over time. Eventually, all the stars would die and all the black holes evaporate away. The Universe would end up cold and barren.

Where is its end?

Most everything that we are familiar with has an inside, an outside, a surface and edges. So, you might ask, where is the edge of the Universe and what is outside of it? The Universe does not have an edge or boundary. This can be a difficult idea to understand because it is so contrary to the world around us and the way we normally think. So let's use our world to help us understand the shape of the Universe. Let's compare the Universe to the surface of the Earth. Where is the end of the surface of the Earth? It has no beginning, end, or even center. Our Universe can be thought of in a similar fashion. It has no beginning, center or end (boundary) in space.

The end

What will eventually happen to the Universe? At this time, we do not know for certain. Astronomers and scientists have to learn more about the Universe and take many more measurements before they can know for certain. Along the way to finally answering this question, they will make more discoveries and there will be surprises: that is, they will discover things about the Universe that they had never thought about. Now, don't get worried about the end of the Universe, because whatever happens, time is on our side.

Glossary

Astronomer. A scientist who studies objects beyond Earth's atmosphere.

Atom. The smallest fundamental unit of matter. There are over 100 different kinds of atoms. The simplest and most abundant is hydrogen. Atoms are made of many sub-atomic particles.

Cloud. A term used loosely in this book to indicate nebulae composed mostly of gaseous hydrogen and helium molecules.

Dust. Dust in space is very much like dust in our homes: specks of solid matter. In space, when enough atoms bond with one another, they can become dust and are large enough to block or reflect light, much like clouds.

Electromagnetic force. One of four forces in nature. This is not the same as electromagnetic radiation. Electromagnetic force is the force associated with the fields of magnets. This type of field can also be generated using electricity. Whenever current is flowing through any electrical wire, a magnetic field is generated around it. Our Earth produces a magnetic field that repels some of the ions emitted by the Sun. The Sun has a strong electromagnetic field produced by the movement of enormous amounts of electrons below its surface.

Electron. Part of an atom that revolves around the nucleus of the atom. The hydrogen atom has one electron. Iron atoms have 26 electrons.

Element. A substance that cannot be further broken down into other substances. An element is composed of one type of atom. Hydrogen, iron, sulfur, aluminum and gold are examples of elements.

Energy. An abstract concept that relates to the ability to produce change or power. Light has the energy to power a calculator or warm an atmosphere. Gasoline has the energy to power cars.

Electromagnetic energy. A form of energy that specifically spans the electromagnetic spectrum.

F or Fahrenheit temperature. The Fahrenheit temperature scale uses 0° F as the lowest temperature that a mixture of water, ice and salt can reach before it freezes; and 212° F for the boiling point of pure water. The United States is one of the few remaining countries that still uses the Fahrenheit scale. Most of the world uses the Celsius temperature scale, where pure water freezes at 0° and boils at 100°. (See page 34)

Fluorescence. The ability of some ions to give off their own light. The best example for this book is ionized hydrogen. A hydrogen atom has one electron. When these atoms are located in nebulae, their electrons can get knocked out of their orbits by highly energetic ultraviolet light radiated from very hot stars. When a hydrogen nucleus recaptures a passing electron, the electron gives off light energy as it "falls" from a high orbit to a more normal lower orbit. Hydrogen fluoresces to produce a faint reddish color.

Gas. One of the three basic states of matter, which are solid, liquid and gas. Gas is the state in which molecules move around the most freely. An example of a gaseous state is our atmosphere on Earth.

Gravity. One of four forces in nature (two of the other forces are atomic and a third is electromagnetic). Gravity is an inherent property of matter that exerts an attraction or pull on matter and energy. The force of gravity increases with mass.

Helium. The second most abundant element or atom in the Universe. Helium is formed from hydrogen in the center of stars .

Hydrogen. The most abundant element or atom in the Universe. About 75% of the matter in the Universe is hydrogen. Hydrogen atoms have a nucleus made of one proton with one electron revolving around it.

Glossary

Image. A likeness of an object or scene that is brought into focus by a telescope or camera. Images are often recorded on photographic film, or obtained from electronic chips such as those used in digital cameras.

Ion. An atom or compound that has a positive or negative charge because it has lost or gained an electron. Ions can fluoresce, that is, they can give off their own light. See Fluorescence.

Light year. A unit of length that is based on the distance that light travels in one year. Light travels at a rate of 186,282 miles per second, so one light year is almost six trillion miles. (See page 34)

M numbers. Many of the objects in this book have designations that begin with a capital M, followed by a number. There is a catalog of 110 celestial objects called Messier Objects, after Charles Messier (1730–1817) who first catalogued them at the end of the 1700s. These are the biggest and brightest objects visible from the northern hemisphere. All can be seen with a small telescope. This is usually the first catalogue of objects that amateur astronomers try to find.

Magnetic. See Electromagnetic Force.

Mass. On Earth, mass is often thought of as weight. Although they are similar, they are not the same thing. Mass is actually the amount of matter or material that makes up an object. In space, all objects are weightless, but they still have mass. In space, it takes a lot more work or energy to move a massive object than a less massive object, even though both weigh nothing.

Matter. Anything made of atoms or parts of atoms. All the physical things around us are made of matter. Electromagnetic energy is not matter, so it is not made of atoms, but it can affect matter (light can heat matter). The Universe is made of matter and energy.

Metal. A special class (or combination) of elements that are made of atoms which can conduct electricity. Metals include aluminum, lead, steel, copper and iron. Steel is a metal made up of several elements.

Molecule. The smallest particle that an element or compound can be divided into. Molecules of elements are often single atoms. Molecules of compounds are several atoms joined or bonded together.

Nucleus of a galaxy. At the very center of every elliptical and spiral galaxy is a nucleus. The highest concentration of stars exists around this area; thus the nucleus is the most massive area of a galaxy. Astronomers think that supermassive black holes reside at the center of most nuclei.

Nebula (plural is nebulae). A giant hydrogen cloud in space where stars and solar systems are often born. The Orion Nebula is one of the best known nebulae and is beautiful to see even in a small telescope.

Photograph. A recording of an image of an object or scene. Images are formed by a telescope, camera lens or other instrument. They are then focused onto photographic film, or a radiation-sensitive electronic chip made up of thousands of tiny squares called pixels.

Scientist. A person who examines and studies the world around us using standardized methods of investigation.

Star/Sun. A sun and a star are the same thing. Our Sun is a star just like all the other stars in the night sky. It appears brighter and larger because we orbit very close to it. Stars produce their energy by nuclear fusion.

Universe. Everything. The space where all the galaxies reside. When you look up at the night sky, you are looking into a part of the Universe.

Weight. See Mass.

Measurements

LENGTH

Abbreviations are in parentheses.

1 inch (in) = 25.4 millimeters exactly; 2.54 centimeters
1 centimeter (cm) = 0.394 inch; 10 millimeters
1 yard (yd) = 0.9144 meters; 36 inches
1 meter (m) = 1.094 yards; 39.37 inches; 100 centimeters; 1,000 millimeters
1 mile (mi) = 1.609344 kilometers; 5,280 feet; 1,760 yards
1 kilometer (km) = 0.621371 miles; 3,281 feet; 1,000 meters
1 astronomical unit (AU) = 92,955,800 miles; 149,597,870 kilometers;
       8.3 light-minutes; this is the average distance from the Earth to the Sun
1 light year (l.y.) = 63,240 astronomical units; almost 6 trillion miles
1 parsec (pc) = 3.26 light years; 206,265 astronomical units (*see below*)

WEIGHT

1 ounce (oz) = 28.35 grams
1 gram (g or gm) = 0.0353 ounces
1 pound (lb) = 0.454 kilograms; 16 ounces
1 kilogram (kg) = 2.205 pounds; 1,000 grams

TEMPERATURE

0° Fahrenheit (F) = −17.8° C; lowest temperature for mixture of water/ice/salt
0° Celsius (C) = 32° F; pure water freezes
212° Fahrenheit = 100° C; pure water boils
Absolute Zero = −459.7° F; −273.16° C; 0K (Kelvin, *see below*); lowest possible temperature

SPEED OF LIGHT

Speed of Light = 186,282 miles/second; 299,792 kilometers/second

The English system versus the Metric system of measurement. The United States is one of the few remaining countries that still uses the English measurement system based on inches, miles, pounds and fluid ounces. The metric system has been adopted by most of the world. Its units of measurement are based on the meter and kilogram, which are evenly divisible by 10. In this book, we decided to use the English system in order to give Americans, the primary readers, a better sense of distances and dimensions, since this is the system they use everyday.

What is a Parsec? A parsec is a unit of length that is often used by astronomers to express the dimensions and distances of galaxies. (Actually, the kiloparsec, a unit of 1,000 parsecs, is used.) A parsec is 3.26 light years and is based on the Astronomical Unit (AU). Understanding how this length was derived involves geometry so we will not explain it here.

Kelvin is a temperature measurement based on Celsius, but it starts at absolute zero instead of the freezing point of pure water. The degree symbol (°) is not used when expressing Kelvin temperatures; only a capital K is placed after the numerical temperature, as in 87K.

Index

Andromeda Galaxy 5-6, 8, 11

Big Bang 5, 7-8, 31
Binary Stars 15
Black Holes 8, 10, 18, 23-25

Cepheid Variables 18
Cosmic Rays 28
Clusters 17

Dark Nebula(e) 16

Electromagnetic Force 32
Electromagnetic Radiation 26-29
Electromagnetic Spectrum 26-29
Elliptical Galaxies 7-8, 10
Emission Nebula(e) 16
Event Horizon 24-25

Galaxies 5, 6-10, 25, 30, 33
Galileo 29
Giant Stars 19, 21
Globular Clusters 17
Gravity 14, 25, 30, 32

Helium 5, 14, 19
Hubble, Edwin 7
Hubble Space Telescope 4, 15, 29
Hydrogen 5, 14, 16, 19

Irregular Galaxies 7-8

Kepler, Johannes 30

Light Year 5, 33

Magellanic Clouds 7, 11
Mass 18-19, 25, 30, 33
Matter & Energy 5, 26
Metric System 34
Milky Way Band 10, 12-13, 28
Milky Way Galaxy 5, 7-8, 10-13, 17
Microwaves 26, 28
Multiple Stars 15
Myths & Legends 13, 17

Nebula(e) 14-6, 22-23 *captions*
Neutron Stars 18, 23, 25
Newton, Isaac 25, 30
Nova(e) 23
Nuclear Fusion 14, 18-19, 21

Orion, *various references to* 15-17

Parsec 34
Planetary Nebula(e) 20-21
Planets 15, 25
Pleiades 17
Pulsars 23

Quasars (*caption*) 24

Radio Telescopes 29
Radioactivity 26
Red Dwarf 21
Red Shift 8
Reflection Nebula(e) 16

Solar System 15
Sound 28
Spectral Lines (caption) 28
Spectrum 8, 26-28
Speed of Light 5, 28
Spiral Galaxies 7, 8, 10
Stars 18-19
    Binaries 15
    Birth 14-15
    Brightness 18
    Clusters 17
    Colors 18
    Death 21-25
    Diameters 18
    Elements 18-19
    Sizes 18
    Temperatures 18
Sun 5, 10, 17-19
Supergiant Stars 19
Supernova(e) 14, 19, 25

Telescopes 29

Ultraviolet Energy/Radiation 16, 21
Universe 5, 7, 31

Variable Stars 18

White Dwarfs 18, 21, 23, 25

X rays 27-29

Contributors

Ken Graun and Suzanne Maly

Ken Graun is the author of the first book in this series, *Our Earth and the Solar System*. He also wrote the popular astronomy field guides, *Touring the Universe* and *What's Out Tonight? 50 Year Astronomy Field Guide, 2000 to 2050*. With David H. Levy, he coauthored the beginner's star chart, *David H. Levy's Guide to the Stars*. Ken lectures and is writing more astronomy books for beginners and children.

Suzanne Maly is an educator for children and adults through the junior college level. She holds a Master in Science degree and has received teaching awards and grants, including an *Arizona Presidential Science Award* and *Energy Lifetime Achievement Award*. Suzanne plans to write other books for children and science education.

Special thanks to Isabelle Houthakker for proofreading and Julianne Hurst-Williams for photography,

Website
VISIT
whatsouttonight.com

Photo Credits

Front cover and dust cover. Background: AURA/NASA/ESA, Galaxy: EUROPEAN SOUTHERN OBSERVATORY, Orion Nebula: BILL SCHOENING/NOAO/AURA/NSF, M87: NASA AND THE HUBBLE HERITAGE TEAM (STSCI/AURA), Planetary nebula: R. SAHAI AND J. TRAUGER (JPL), THE WFPC2 SCIENCE TEAM AND NASA. Back cover and dust cover: EUROPEAN SOUTHERN OBSERVATORY. *Inside front dust cover.* R. SAHAI AND J. TRAUGER (JPL), THE WFPC2 SCIENCE TEAM AND NASA. *Inside back dust cover.* JULIANNE HURST-WILLIAMS. *Front end pages.* Galaxies: AURA/NASA/ESA, Group of galaxies: HUBBLE HERITAGE TEAM (AURU/STSCI/NASA), Elliptical galaxy: NOAO/AURA/NSF, Spiral galaxy: BILL SCHOENING/NOAO/AURA/NSF, Orion Nebula: BILL SCHOENING/NOAO/AURA/NSF, Trifid Nebula: NASA AND JEFF HESTER, Large cluster: NASA, ESA, AND MARTINO ROMANIELLO (EUROPEAN SOUTHERN OBSERVATORY, GERMANY0, Small cluster: N.A. SHARP, MARK HANNA, REU PROGRAM/NOAO/AURA/NSF, Planetary nebula: NASA AND THE HUBBLE HERITAGE TEAM (STSCI/AURA), Supernova: NASA AND THE HUBBLE HERITAGE TEAM (STSCI/AURA). *Back end pages.* KEN GRAUN. *Page 1.* EUROPEAN SOUTHERN OBSERVATORY. *Page 3.* JULIANNE HURST-WILLIAMS. *Page 4.* AURA/NASA/ESA. *Page 5.* Galaxy: BILL SCHOENING, VANESSA HARVEY/REU PROGRAM/NOAO/AURA/NSF, Moon: KEN GRAUN. *Page 7.* Elliptical galaxy: NOAO/AURA/NSF, Spiral galaxy: TODD BOROSON/NOAO/AURA/NSF. *Page 8.* Irregular galaxy: NASA, ESA, R. DE GRIJS (INSTITUTE OF ASTRONOMY, CAMBRIDGE, UK), Sombrero galaxy: TODD BOROSON/NOAO/AURA/NSF. *Page 9.* MIKE PIERCE, JOHN JURCEVIC (INDIANA)/WIYN/NOAO/NSF. *Page 10.* Top: EUROPEAN SOUTHERN OBSERVATORY Bottom: NASA/COBE/DIRBE, Inset: NASA. *Page 11.* AURA/NOAO/NSF. *Page 12.* DAVID TALENT/AURU/NOAO/NSF. *Page 14/15.* Eagle Nebula: BILL SCHOENING/AURA/NOAO/NSF, Three Pillars of Creation images: JEFF HESTER AND PAUL SCOWEN (ARIZONA STATE UNIVERSITY) AND NASA, Orion Nebula: BILL SCHOENING/NOAO/AURA/NSF. *Page 16/17.* Clockwise from Horsehead Nebula: N.A. SHARP/NOAO/AURA/NSF, N.A. SHARP, REU PROGRAM/NOAO/AURA/NSF, N.A. SHARP, REU PROGRAM/NOAO/AURA/NSF, ANGLO-AUSTRALIAN OBSERVATORY/ROYAL OBSERVATORY EDINBURGH, NOAO/AURA/NSF. *Page 18.* Top: A. DUPREE (CFA), NASA, ESA, Bottom graphics by KEN GRAUN. *Page 19.* Graphics by KEN GRAUN. *Page 20.* Clockwise from top left: NASA AND THE HUBBLE HERITAGE TEAM (STSCI/AURA), WIYN/NOAO/NSF, NASA AND THE HUBBLE HERITAGE TEAM (STSCI/AURA), J.P. HARRINGTON AND K.J. BORKOWSKI (UNIVERSITY OF MARYLAND), AND NASA. *Page 21.* Top: R. SAHAI AND J. TRAUGER (JPL), THE WFPC2 SCIENCE TEAM AND NASA., Bottom: NOAO/AURA/NSF. *Page 22.* Main: JAY GALLAGHER (U. WISCONSIN)/WIYN/NOAO/NSF, Inset: NASA AND THE HUBBLE HERITAGE TEAM (STSCI/AURA). *Page 23.* Top: AURA/STSCI/NASA, Bottom: N.A. SHARP, REU PROGRAM/NOAO/AURA/NSF. *Page 24.* Clockwise: NASA AND THE HUBBLE HERITAGE TEAM (STSCI/AURA), NASA/ESA/HST, NASA AND JEFFREY KENNEY AND ELIZABETH YALE (YALE UNIVERSITY), NASA AND JEFFREY KENNEY AND ELIZABETH YALE (YALE UNIVERSITY). *Page 25.* Clip art from PHOTODISC. *Page 26/27.* Spectrum along bottom of pages: KEN GRAUN. *Page 27.* Top left: AURA/NOAO/NSF, Top right: NRAO/AUI, Bottom: NASA/CXC/SAO. *Page 28.* Top: NASA, Bottom: NIGEL SHARP, NOAO/AURA/NSF. *Page 29.* Top to bottom: NASA, NASA, MARK HANNA/NOAO/AURA/NSF, DAVE FINLEY, DAVID PARKER. *Page 31.* AURA/NASA/ESA. *Page 36.* JULIANNE HURST-WILLIAMS.

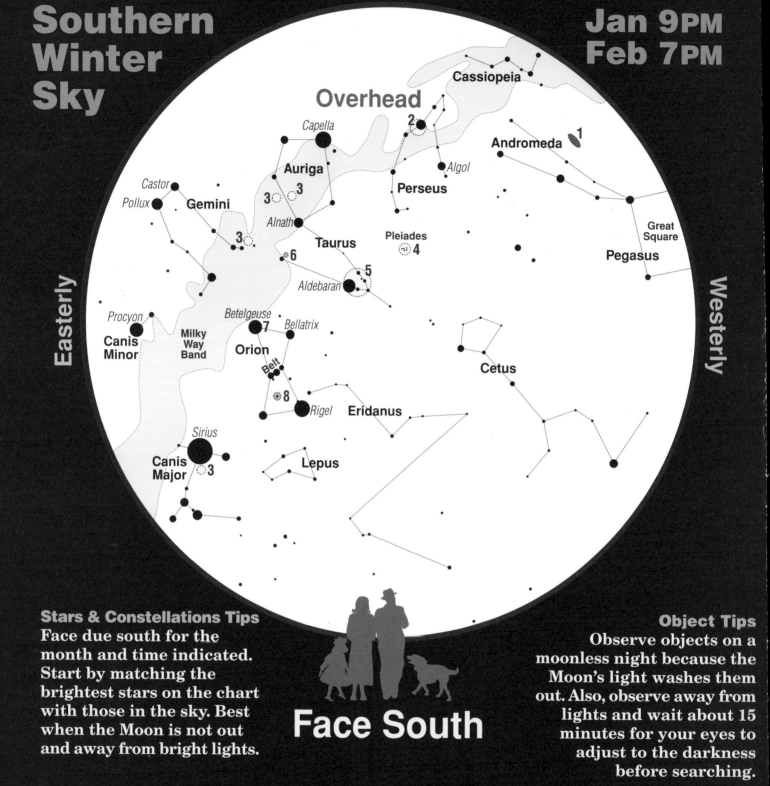

Southern Winter Sky

Jan 9PM
Feb 7PM

Overhead

Cassiopeia

Andromeda

Capella

2

Auriga

Algol

Perseus

Castor

3 *3*

Pollux

Gemini

Alnath

Pleiades

4

Great Square

Taurus

3

6

Pegasus

5

Aldebaran

Easterly

Westerly

Procyon

Betelgeuse

Bellatrix

Canis Minor

Milky Way Band

Orion

7

Belt

Cetus

8

Rigel

Eridanus

Sirius

Lepus

Canis Major

3

Face South

Stars & Constellations Tips
Face due south for the month and time indicated. Start by matching the brightest stars on the chart with those in the sky. Best when the Moon is not out and away from bright lights.

Object Tips
Observe objects on a moonless night because the Moon's light washes them out. Also, observe away from lights and wait about 15 minutes for your eyes to adjust to the darkness before searching.

1. Andromeda Galaxy. Use binoculars. (page 6)

2. Nice loose star cluster that comes alive with binoculars.

3. Four star clusters best seen with telescope around 50x. Try with binoculars.

4. Pleiades visible with eyes but best with binoculars. (page 16/17)

5. Hyades is a large old cluster best viewed with eyes.

6. Crab Nebula supernova explosion. Need dark skies & telescope at 40x to 100x. (page 22)

7. The supergiant star Betelgeuse. (page 18)

8. Orion Nebula is *great* with small telescope at 40x to 100x. (page 15)